C0-AKC-567

SALVATORE FERRAGAMO

First published in the United States of America in 2000
by UNIVERSE PUBLISHING
A Division of Rizzoli International Publications, Inc.
300 Park Avenue South
New York, NY 10010

and

THE VENDOME PRESS

Copyright © 2000 by Éditions Assouline, Paris
Translated from the French by Cynthia Calder

All rights reserved. No part of this publication may be reproduced, stored in a retrieval system, or transmitted in any form or by any means, electronic, mechanical, photocopying,
recording, or otherwise, without prior consent of the publishers
ISBN: 0-7893-0469-4

Color Separation: Gravor (Switzerland)
Printed and bound in Italy

Library of Congress Catalog Card Number: TK

2000 2001 2002 2003 / 10 9 8 7 6 5 4 3 2 1

SALVATORE FERRAGAMO

BY FRANÇOIS BAUDOT

UNIVERSE

If you believe that "the early bird gets the worm", then it will come as no surprise that the name of Salvatore Ferragamo is recognized all over the world. Remarkable talent might not have been enough to assure success for the modest cobbler from Bonito. However, that talent combined with courage and tenacity, an excellent business sense and an innate grasp of the international market allowed him, and later his descendants, to establish one of the few global luxury brands that remains under the founding family's control. The history of the company evolved over the course of several decades and two generations, with a handful of determined men and women, the encouragement of some prominent individuals, support from the press and a popular appeal which never diluted the quality of Ferragamo's increasingly diversified product line.

Behind this success, there is a real man and a modern fairy tale that is recalled by his admirers when they remember Salvatore Ferragamo. He was a true sculptor, whose fingers molded thousands of forms, wondrous little sculptures to fit the feet of the most wealthy and famous women. His personal legend embodies the Italian dream that meshes so perfectly with American philosophy. Half Cinderella story, half triumph of free enterprise, it is the true story of a cobbler on a quest to conquer the new world. The young emigrant who became the shoemaker to the stars. For Salvatore, reality often surpassed fantasy. The remarkable development of the brand named after him is an eloquent testimony.

Sadly, Salvatore Ferragamo never had the chance to see his brand mature. Though he was continuosly one step ahead of the times, anticipating trends from past fashions, seizing opportunities and moving beyond them, the fate he had so effectively challenged caught up with him at the age of sixty-two years. He was gone too soon, but the magical shoemaker nevertheless bequeathed a substantial heritage. It is difficult to believe that in less than half a century, a single man could conceive so many variations and developments in footwear. The Salvatore Ferragamo Museum, open to the public on the third floor of the Palazzo Spini Ferroni, the Ferragamo company headquarters, redesigns its display cases every two years based on a new theme, drawing on its reserve collection of ten thousand different models. Some are prototypes, and others have shod the feet of celebrities. Many have contributed to a star's allure, a film's success, a fashion trend or a distinctively stylish gait. Some have become classics that were, and still are, imitated all over the world.

Such endlessly inventive forms would even strike those with little interest in fashion or its accessories. The experimentation, the variety, the new directions taken in the art of women's shoe design

6

match the height of Parisian haute couture in their elegance. But this family story actually began in America, unfolding like the plot of a film.

directed by Cecil B. De Mille in 1923, the first version of the *Ten Commandments*, a biblical epic film, dazzled the entire world. The attention devoted to the decor and costumes of this masterpiece of silent film contributed greatly to its success. The sandals worn in the film were particularly notable. As a novice shoemaker, Salvatore Ferragamo plunged into the history of antique art to come up with the designs for the Pharaoh and captives. He personally made the shoes that Moses wore to lead the people to the promised land. For the young cobbler this was his first step towards success. In America at that time, women's ankles were still hidden inside ankle-high boots, the object of erotic desire. The high laced buskins featured in the film suddenly launched a liberating trend in fashion. The demand for sandals boomed and the name of the designer of this new shoe style was heard on everyone's lips. He was known as the little Italian cobbler with the shop near the studios.

Three-quarters of a century later, in 1992, when the Los Angeles County Museum dedicated a retrospective to the "Shoemaker to the Stars", Charlton Heston, who played Moses in the second version of the most famous trip across the desert, naturally chose to visit the Ferragamo family for the occasion at the Rodeo Drive boutique. But what a lot had happened between the making of those two films!

Originally from Bonito, a village outside Naples, the Ferragamo family had faithfully worked the land for several generations. The family to which Salvatore was born in 1898 was one of the most humble. He was born the eleventh of fourteen children. One by one, his brothers and sisters crossed the Atlantic to try their luck. Their stories were not unlike the great emigrant adventure that Charlie Chaplin - he was to become a friend of Salvatore's - acted out in movie houses, evoking both laughter and tears. Even though life in Bonito was tough, cultivating the land had its noble side. It was the peasant who brought in the harvest and made him an important member of society. Thus Salvatore's father was confused about his youngest son's insistent desire to apprentice himself to the village cobbler. From an early age, he was fixated on one idea: to make shoes. At the age of four he played with pieces of leather, putting together and taking apart the wooden clogs that the old cobbler hammered out under the boy's watchful gaze - a scene straight from the workshop of Gepetto. Under the Neapolitan caste system the cobbler probably held the lowest rank on the social ladder. Salvatore's father had to resolve his crisis. At nine the boy had finished his primary studies and since neither his family nor the local area could offer him anything further, he was sent to work as an apprentice for the best shoemaker in Naples. He accomplished the job without complaint. The local clientele were extremely demanding for there, at the base of Mt. Vesuvius, much importance was placed on footwear. Many dandies felt incomplete unless they were well-heeled. Of course, their livelihood did not depend on shoes.

In 1910, after Salvatore turned twelve, he had learned enough to return to his village where he opened his first workshop. The little Ferragamo boy employed two workers with whom he fashioned his first custom-made shoes. By the time he was sixteen his parents could no longer prevent him from joining his siblings in California.

8

In 1915 Salvatore Ferragamo opened a tiny boutique in Santa Barbara along the road where the American Film Company and other businesses were already engaged in their ruthless pursuit. As movie stars passed by on their way to making films and winning fame, their attention was drawn to his shop. No order or feat was too great for him, nothing discouraged him. Mere youngsters themselves, some of the greatest celebrities stopped in: Mary Pickford, her attractive husband Douglas Fairbanks, Pola Negri, Rudolf Valentino's fiancèe, and the mankiller herself Gloria Swanson, soon to become the Marquise de la Falaise, one of the most elegant women in American cinema. All of these rising stars forged friendships with Ferragamo that reflected the American democratic ideal. It meant much to this modest southern Italian that he could develop relationships with some of the most famous people, solely on the basis of his merits. He knew this could not happen anywhere else but in America.

by the beginning of the 1920s, although the film business was not yet fully established, Salvatore already knew that his destiny would be forever intertwined with the film industry. As a world of illusions and a means of production, the cinema fascinated him. Against his brothers' advice he moved premises and set up shop, this time in the heart of Hollywood on Las Palmas. The location of the greatest dream factory of the century. Salvatore was to experience both its success and its pressures. He shared the doubts and triumphs. His business took off with the popularity of spectacle films, epics that made a mark on the world which deeply influenced both the ethics and the aesthetics of the twentieth century. In its humble way, the house of Ferragamo gained a certain authority in cinema. Salvatore was the right person at the right time. And he had the sense to seize the moment The trick was to make his luck last. In order to fully exercise his art though, a shoemaker must forge relationships with his clientele that penetrate deeper than those of the general supplier. Acting the role of accomplice and confidante, confessor and advisor, Salvatore used his skills to charm, negotiate, suggest and battle with each personality, fighting for the shape of the materials, the style that he believed best suited each individual. It is said that Don Juan held thousands of women in his arms. According to this Leporello of the shoe, he held the most beautiful feet in the world between his palms: duchesses, maharanis, prima donnas, film, theater and ballet stars. From large personalities to tiny women, from nightingales to black swans, mothers and daughters alike, Salvatore loved each of them in his own way, shodding them as he saw fit. He was happy dedicating his superb craftsmanship to their adornment. By the time he turned forty he realized that he had not spent enough time perfecting his own foothold. From the beginning of his career, Salvatore Ferragamo had weighed his abilities and assessed his faults. After he had established himself in Hollywood he enrolled at the University of Los Angeles where he studied comparative anatomy. He took courses that taught him about the individual bones of the foot, as well as the skeleton and the balance and movement of the body. He learned the subtleties of this most complex of architectural structures. He found that all the weight of a woman's body, and the center of balance and stability, fall on the arc that the shoe forms under the arch of the foot. The study of this curve, in all its variables, became a life-long pursuit. It yielded prototypes that were remarkable for their special elegance as well as their comfort, offering his clients a feeling of comfort, ease and support, essential elements of style. Salvatore Ferragamo believed there was no limit to the materials a shoemaker could use to shod his female clients. His repertoire included diamonds and pearls (real and false), antelope, kangaroo, leopard, python or water snakeskin, the first plastics and transparent nylon thread for "invisible" shoes. The shoemaker made footwear from plaited raffia, a delicate technique exclusive to the villages around Florence, and crocheted materials, a craft for which this area was also known, while borrowing others' techniques such as Chinese brocades, Egyptian linens, Indian silks, Cordovan leathers. His boundless innovation led him to design the light-weight cork platform sole. Although this shoe inspired many copies the world over, he personally derived the greatest benefit from his invention. He was also the first to create a collapsible heel allowing elegant women a whimsical way of changing shoes to suit their fancy.

f erragamo also delved into researching the use of fish skins, a novel material in the shoe industry. He was particularly interested in the shark scales that ranged in color from subtle shades of dark blue to light silver. In his creations he often employed fanciful and unconventional alternatives, juxtaposing the precious with the savage, placing rustic elements side by side with extravagant materials, combining feminine and masculine touches. Historical references were used to produce futuristic creations. The final product: a tiny carousel, chiseled like a jewel but as functional as an instrument.

In addition to studying anatomy, art history and the effect of artistic trends in modernity, this self-taught man took courses in mathema

11

tics with the goal of perfecting his work. He also audited classes in physics and chemistry. From these studies he pioneered new materials, skin processing techniques and color chemistry. They also led to the introduction of revolutionary approaches in the realm of footwear such as the processing of ultra-light cellophane resulting in a wonderful material for summer shoes. The shoemaker's inspiration for this technique came from the rustling of a candy wrapper. Other innovations included high heels fashioned in fine openwork metal. Transparent vinyl soles, delicate woven lace vamps, petit point work, hand-painted leathers, braided grosgrain ribbon, rainbow color applications, suede on suede, Venetian glass bead motifs and delicate Oriental embroidery - he satisfied his public with a vast array of fanciful creations.

by the end of the 1920s, Salvatore Ferragamo's name no longer reigned over shoe design in Hollywood alone. Orders came from all over the United States. This posed a difficult problem for the shoemaker who felt the country lacked sufficient workers to expand his luxury craft and still maintain the standard of quality he demanded. In 1927, homesick and needing to respond to increased business, Salvatore chose to return home. Or at least as far as Florence, where he established his company headquarters. The shoemaker felt that the city was not only one of the most prestigious in Italy, but also that it would offer the best craftsmen for his needs. He had not yet introduced any mechanization in his workshops. Each worker specialized in a specific task. Everyone worked at being the best in his skill. Every step involved in the luxury shoemaking process was done by hand. Known for his hands-on approach, Salvatore never let a detail slide. Nothing escaped his careful inspection. Still working on his versatility, he always had his eye out for new shapes and materials. All the while he remained the best public relations resource in the house. As the company continued to grow, it was he who always received the clients, among them, the most celebrated in the world, and who supervised the management of the business with the same careful attention. Just after the second world war, along with the American clientele, he began to receive elegant Europeans, including many rich and beautiful Italians who had discovered his hallowed name that carried with it the prestige of Hollywood.

In 1950, the house of Ferragamo employed seven hundred and fifty people producing an average of three hundred and fifty pairs of hand-made shoes every day. The day had come when Italian cinema studios were ready to rival those of Hollywood. Having been drained by the war, Italy was now rid of fascism and prepared, with the help of the United States, to redeploy its energy. In the fashion arena, Paris, the capital of haute couture, would now have to contend with the Italians. To the long list of Hollywood stars conquered by Salvatore including Lauren Bacall, Ava Gardner, Katherine Hepburn, Joan Crawford, Claudette Colbert, Paulette Goddard, Marilyn Monroe, were introduced the new candidates. Among the Latin beauties Sophia Loren embodied the curvaceous figurehead. Others that came forward included the "very rich and very thin grandes dames" such as the Duchess of Windsor, Soraya, "the princess with the sad eyes", and international stars like Greta Garbo and Ingrid Bergman. Young newcomers also entered the scene , such as the delicious Audrey Hepburn. During *Roman Holiday*, the house of Ferragamo made a ballerina slipper for "sweet" Audrey that traveled around the world. Audrey was never to forget Salvatore.

Glamour emanates for the most part from the self-assurance of a good person. This is even more obvious on the screen, on the stage and in public appearances where a star can never take a false step. But Ferragamo was not content just to shod his clients. He guaranteed that they would never have to worry about their feet, a certificate of good business. This assurance was one of the main secrets behind the popularity of his shoes, made for one of the most versatile group of clients of the 20th century.

the height of success lies in the ability to share it. Sacrifices become important when they are made for a goal. Success was not enough to motivate the last of the Ferragamos. He had acquired a comfortable lifestyle, gained shoe after shoe, day after day, dollar after dollar for twenty years. In 1940, Bonito needed a hospice. The doctor of the village, who was also the mayor, called home the prodigal son. Salvatore financed everything without a blink. He returned to his village for the inauguration where he was greeted warmly by the mayor who introduced his daughter to Salvatore. The shoemaker to the stars had met his mate. He had not yet lived a full life or found true happiness. Wanda Miletti was eighteen, with a good head on her shoulders, having received a solid education from the ladies of the Sacred Convent. She offered several vague bumbling compliments to the generous donor who did not respond. He observed her. Then, turning to one of her sisters he said: "That women will be my wife!" They were to have six children together. "I was a young provincial bourgeois girl. I had been raised properly which meant that I had no sense of reality. When I understood the efforts undertaken by my future husband to get to his position in life, when slowly but surely he revealed to me all the sacrifices he had endured, when I understood his profound honesty, his loyalty, his human respect, I loved him more and more. That is why after his death in 1960, I continued to fight every challenge. So that his company would survive him. At that time, I did not even know how to sign a check but I always had my feet on the ground. I have had instilled in me the respect for money and the prudence that you need for the future and to maintain the family. Once my husband was gone, we all banded together to work. It took ten years. That was how long it was before Ferruccio, my oldest son, finished his secondary studies and turned twenty, at which time he was prepared to take over the management of the business. On the other hand, Fiamma, my oldest child and the only one who had been able to work with her father, though only for a short time at the age of seventeen, devoted her attention to designing shoes." She presented her first full collection in London in 1961, a great success! From that time to her death, also premature, in 1998, Fiamma coordinated all the leather lines. In 1978 she was named "Designer of the Year" by *Footwear News*.

Epilogue

Wanda Ferragamo seems at peace today. Since Salvatore's day, the company's shoe production has changed considerably. Mechanization was slowly introduced into the production of luxury shoes and as shoes were sold in each half size, and new machines appeared with advanced technology, their sophistication rendered hand-made shoes obsolete. The daily quantity of shoes produced today under the Salvatore Ferragamo label has reached several ten thousand pairs of men's and ladies' shoes.

Having become the Marquise de San Giuliano, Fiamma, who joined the governing board of the Bank of Italy, remained largely responsible for the expansion of the family business. Her sister Giovanna, who was only fifteen in 1958, entered the shoe design side and presented her first full ready-to-wear line at the Pitti Palace in Florence. She accomplished one of her father's goals which was to diversify the shoemaking activities in order to create a global universe for the Ferragamo name. This is the concept that currently drives the majority of European luxury houses. Since then, the Ferragamo house has presented its own fashion collections every season at the ready-to-wear show in Milan. Giovanna always supervises all the models. The third of the Ferragamo girls, Fulvia Visconti, began to structure the Accessories Division in 1971. She focused on the production of silk scarves and establishing the name in Milan, which had become the center of Italian fashion. In addition to Ferruccio, the Chief Executive Officer of the

Salvatore Ferragamo group, of which Wanda remains Chairman, Leonardo joined this strong family business in his twenties, developing the European and Asian markets, and later managing the diversification of the group and its activities. Finally, Massimo, the youngest of the second generation of Ferragamos, took over the American branch of the business. The US market, where this famiglia business was born, accounts for 40% of sales. This represented a consolidated market worth 805 billion lira in 1999. There are over one hundred Ferragamo boutiques, where the ladies' shoe remains the key seller with over 30% of global sales. The lessons of the little Neapolitan artisan still holds. His tradition carries on while many new ideas continue to enter the door of the house he founded.

The Ferragamos, with the third generation already entering the business, continue to rise early. How can they match their parents efforts, if they don't try to work even harder?

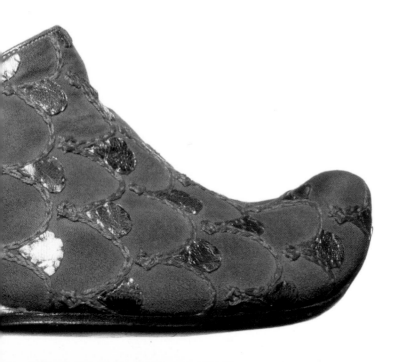

Duchella Windsor

Greta Garbo

FIG.1

FIG.2

FIG.3

FIG.4

FIG.5

FIG.6

FIG.7

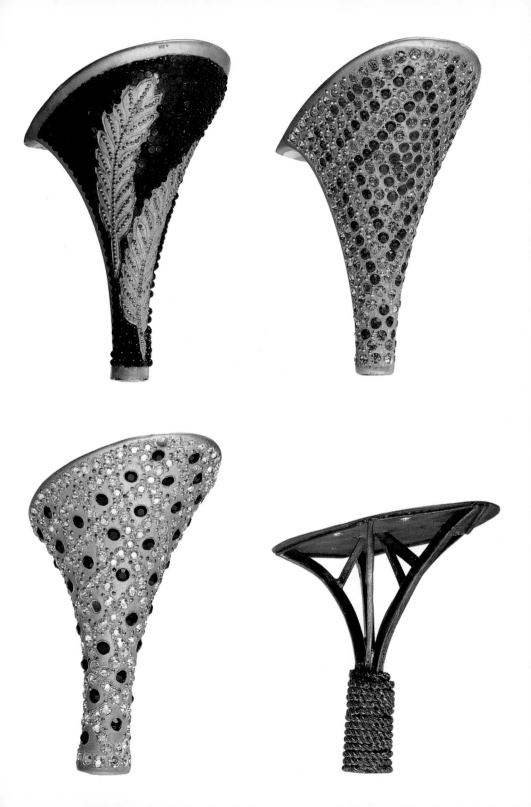

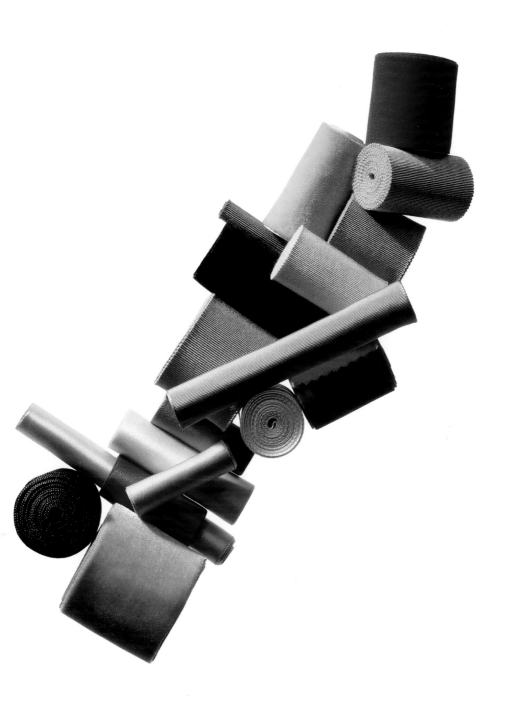

Chronology

1898 : Salvatore Ferragamo is born on June 5 in Bonito, a village near Naples.

1914 : Apprenticed to a cobbler at the age of nine, Salvatore Ferragamo immigrates to the United States in the summer of 1914 to join his brothers and open a shoe shop in Santa Barbara (1033 State Street). His American career begins. By sixteen he is working for the American Film Co.

1920 : He enrolls in anatomy courses at the University of Santa Barbara.

1923 : Cecil B. De Mille asks him to create the sandals and costumes for the film *The Ten Commandments*. He is an immediate sensation. The film industry moves to Hollywood and Salvatore Ferragamo opens a shop on Hollywood Boulevard. He crafts fabulous shoes for Gloria Swanson, Joan Crawford and Mary Pickford, and designs the first sandals.

1927 : Salvatore Ferragamo decides to return to Italy and establishes his workshop in Florence.

1933 : Following the 1929 stock market crash in the United States, his business goes bankrupt and is then revived with more focus on the Italian clientele.

1936 : This is an intensive period of creativity during which he invents the cork soles and launches his famous ultra-light "Wedgies", copied the world over.

1938 : He acquires the Palazzo Spini Feroni, a 13th century Florentine building, which becomes the Ferragamo company headquarters.

1940: Salvatore Ferragamo marries Wanda Miletti, daughter of the mayor of Bonito, with whom he has six children, Fiamma, Giovanna, Ferruccio, Fulvia, Leonardo, Massimo.

1947 : He receives the Neiman Marcus Oscar for his "invisible" sandal made of nylon thread and for his contribution to fashion.His most faithful clients include: Marilyn Monroe, Audrey Hepburn, Rita Hayworth, Greta Garbo, Sophia Loren and the international beau monde.

1949 : He collaborates with Christian Dior and Elsa Schiaparelli.

1951 : He participates in his first Italian fashion show in Florence and creates the *Kimo* sandal inspired by Japanese *tabi*.

1952 : He invents the glove arch and the cage heel (1952) and works on an 18-karat gold sandal (1956).

1955 : He begins to produce *Ferrina* and *Ferragamo Debs* shoes, introducing some machine-made operations. Industrialization has begun

1958 : Fiamma Ferragamo begins working with her father.

Three-quarter length raincoat in dark blue suede, "Shada" boot in black elastic lycra with a suede heel and patent leather sole.
fall/winter collection 2000-2001© Photo Patrick Demarchelier.

1959 : At the age of sixteen, Giovanna Ferragamo presents her first ready-to-wear "Resort" line.

1960 : Salvatore Ferragamo dies on August 7. His wife, Wanda Ferragamo, takes over the business, adding diverse lines to the house (from shoes to the total look) with the help of her children.

1965 : Giovanna Ferragamo presents her first full ready-to-wear line in the White Room of the Pitti Palace. A line of bags and suitcases is introduced.

1967 : Fiamma receives the Neiman Marcus Oscar for her shoe creations, twenty years after her father.

1971 : Fulvia Visconti Ferragamo develops the silk accessories line (ties and scarves).

1974 : Men's ready-to-wear is introduced.

1985 : Salvatore Ferragamo retrospective show at the Strozzi Palace.

1992 : Retrospective show at the Los Angeles County Museum. The Ferragamo name is introduced in France with the opening of flagship boutiques in Paris and other major French cities.

1995 : Inauguration of the Salvatore Ferragamo Museum in Florence, in the Palazzo Spini Feroni.

1996 : The Ferragamo group takes over the prestigious house of Emmanuel Ungaro.

1998 : Exhibition in Tokyo celebrating the one-hundredth year of Salvatore Ferragamo's birth. Launch of the first perfume, *Salvatore Ferragamo pour femme*, and a line of sunglasses.

2000 : The men's perfume is awarded Men's Fragrance of the Year at the 28th edition of the American FIFI Awards.

High-heeled suede patchwork boot.

Fall /Winter Collection 2000 © Photo Patrick Demarchelier.

Salvatore Ferragamo

The Palazzo Spini Feroni in Florence. This medieval building, acquired by Salvatore Ferragamo in 1938, is the company headquarters.© Salvatore Ferragamo Museum, Florence.
Portrait of Salvatore Ferragamo by Pietro Annigoni (1949), which represents the shoemaker as an artist. © Salvatore Ferragamo Museum, Florence.

Salvatore Ferragamo's workshop in the Alcove room, once the Bagnano family bedroom, decorated with 18th century frescoes by Ranieri del Pace. Palazzo Spini Feroni, 1937. © Photo Alinari Archives, Florence.

A model from the beginning of the 1930s that mirrors the influences of art and the Hollywood period. Hand-painted kidskin. © Photo Christopher Broabent.
Salvatore Ferragamo in Hollywood at the beginning of the 1920s, where he began his career © Photo Archives Alinari, Florence.

Black velvet sandal embroidered with silver kidskin, open heel formed with three gold and silver kidskin straps, silver kid-covered flat wooden sole joined the high heel to the cork platform covered in alternating layers of silver and gold kidskin. 1938-1939.
Sandal in gold kidskin, brass high heel formed in cubes of decreasing size to evoke the shape of the pyramids. 1930. © Photos Massimo Listri.

Publicity drawings by the futuristic painter Lucio Venna for Salvatore Ferragamo, 1930. The shoemaker was influenced by the artistic atmosphere of the period. © Salvatore Ferragamo Museum, Florence.
Closed shoe in white suede with leaf applications of pink, blue, yellow and green suede, 1930. **Laced shoe in black suede**, with geometric green, yellow, pink and blue applications, 1930. © Photos Roberto Quagli.

Sandal in gold and silver kidskin (two cross-over bands) Roman strap, metal buckle, three-layered cork platform sole covered in Bakelite and gold kid, transparent cylindrical Bakelite heel, 1940. © Photo Christopher Broabent.

Shoes with Oriental toes. Red suede and gold kid mules, cork platform heel, 1938. "Goccia" mule with powder blue suede vamp, decorated with gold kid, embroidered and edged with pink silk point de chainette, 1948-1950. © Photos Christopher Broabent.

Hand-painted fabric pump, evoking the blue tones of sailing ships, square heel and tip, high heel in blue fabric-covered wood, 1930-1935. © Photo Christopher Broabent.
Publicity drawings by Riccardo Magni, published by Bellezza in December 1945. © Photo Umberto Visentini.

Multi-colored raffia crocheted sandal, flat heel formed from four corks, 1935-1936. Straw and raffia were some of his most successful materials, used for both beach shoes and more sophisticated city models. The popularity of these materials was attributed to their low price and light weight. Although they had been used by Florentine artisans since the 18th century, Salvatore Ferragamo was the first Italian to use them for shoes. © Photo Christopher Broabent.

Salvatore and Wanda Ferragamo with their six children. From left to right: Giovanna, Fulvia, Fiamma, Leonardo, Ferruccio and Massimo. All of the Ferragamo children are involved in the family business, 1959. © Photo from Historic Locchi Archives, Florence.

"Invisible" Sandal. A single nylon thread was passed from one side of the insole to the other, a system held in by an ankle strap, with an "F"-shape green kid-covered wooden wedge heel, 1947. The shoe was created for the Neiman Marcus Award. Ferragamo's idea was inspired by watching fishermen on the Arno river from his window in the Palazzo Spini Ferroni. © Photo Christopher Broabent. Right, the model was presented in L'Europeo, April 17, 1947.

Gold and silver kid sandal, Roman strap, cork sole and heel, red velvet heel with hand-worked brass and rhinestone, 1938. Model made for the Maharani of Cooch Behar. © Photo Christopher Broabent.
"Viva" and Michouette" sandals. Pale yellow satin embroidered with cylindrical Venetian glass beads and topaz rhinestone, 1968; crimson satin embroidered with gold and silver Venetian beads, oval-shaped topaz and ruby-colored rhinestones, 1968. © Photo Sergio Merli.

Sandal brocaded in gold and green silk with floral motifs, upper embroidered with two gold kid bands forming a center knot, bright green mica-covered high stiletto heel with transparent vinyl sole, 1955. © Photo Christopher Broabent. **Salvatore Ferragamo** looking through the vinyl portion of the sole of one of his most famous shoes from the 1950s., 1955. © Photo from historic Locchi Archives, Florence.

Ferragamo in Bellezza (January 1950), presenting the designs for shoes worn by the Duchess of Windsor and Greta Garbo. © Photo Umberto Visentini.

18-karat gold sandal, shaped into two linked necklaces, Roman strap, engraved gold-covered high heel overlaid with a dragon motif, 1956. Sandal made for an Australian client. © Photo Christopher Broabent.

Patent for the "cage" heel, January 7, 1956. Made with filigreed metal, usually brass, the cage was hollow or encased a smaller heel made from another material. The framework connected the sole to the top of the heel. © Photo Roberto Quagli / Salvatore Ferragamo Museum, Florence.

"Calypso" sandal, upper composed of three black satin bands, brass "cage" stiletto heel, 1955-56. © Photo Christopher Broabent.

Ferragamo among the thousands of wooden lasts belonging to his famous clients, 1950. © Photo from Historic Locchi Archives, Florence.

Brown crocodile pump, high stiletto heel, 1958-59. Shoe created for Marilyn Monroe. © Photo Christopher Broabent.

The famous shoes made for Marilyn Monroe between 1956 and 1960, each with an 11 cm heel. They were purchased from the Christie's Marilyn sale in New York in October 1999. © Photo Roberto Quagli.

Marilyn Monroe in *The Seven Year Itch*, directed by Billy Wilder in 1955. She was one of Salvatore Ferragamo's most famous clients. © Rue des Archives, Paris.

"Damigella" boot in white elasticated silk with a gold brocade effect, gold kid-covered wooden stiletto heel, 1955-1956. Model designed for Sophia Loren. © Photo Christopher Broabent.

Ferragamo heels made during the 1950s. © Photo Roberto Quagli.

Salvatore Ferragamo with Sophia Loren in Rome in 1955. © Photo Del Vecchio et Scala.

Ballerina slippers made for Audrey Hepburn by Salvatore Ferragamo from 1954 to 1965, with "shell" soles. © Photo Roberto Quagli.

Salvatore Ferragamo and Audrey Hepburn at the Palazzo Spini Feroni in 1954. © Photo from Historic Locchi Archives, Florence.

Fiamma Ferragamo photographed by David Lees in 1967 for Life. © Photo David Lees / Salvatore Ferragamo Museum, Florence. **Ankle boot with white kid straps and "Pleja" sandal.** Orange crocheted ("pontovo") synthetic raffia, 1966; yellow crocheted synthetic raffia, yellow kid-covered sculpted wooden trapezoid heel with hollow center, calf ankle strap. This second model by Fiamma Ferragamo won the Neiman Marcus Award in 1967. © Photo Roberto Quagli.

"Vara", Ferragamo's most famous shoe for the last twenty years, designed by Fiamma Ferragamo in 1978, with a signature gray grosgrain ribbon . © Photo Sergio Merli.
The famous grosgrain Ferragamo ribbon used for shoes, ready-to-wear and luggage. © Photo Roberto Quagli.

Zebra boot decorated with black calf buckled straps, oval heel, 1964-1965. © Photo Roberto Quagli.
Fiamma Ferragamo among her creations, 1965. © Photo from Historic Locchi Archives, Florence.

Pink satin moccasin, embroidered "Marguerite" square toe (beads with Venetian glass baguettes and rhinestone), pink satin-covered Louis XV heel, 1967. © Photo Roberto Quagli. **Moiré taffeta and pearl grey silk organza mule** embroidered with transparent glass beads, tiny smoke glass baguettes and white Swarovski beads, Plexiglass heel decorated with silver and rhinestone filigree. Model created for the 1998 Andy Tennant film, *Ever After*, A Cinderella Story. © Photo Roberto Quagli.

"Audrey" ballerina slippers with "shell" sole, 2000 spring-summer collection. Copies of the model created by Salvatore Ferragamo for Audrey Hepburn in 1954. © Photo Roberto Quagli.

Scarves and printed silks were added to the Ferragamo collection in the 1960s, becoming one of the most important symbols of the Italian house. The drawings on silk are inspired primarily by flowers and animals. 1987 spring-summer collection.

"Capri" motif for a printed silk scarf: butterflies, flowers and shoes from the Salvatore Ferragamo Museum. 1996 spring-summer collection. © Photo Giovanni Gastel. **"Gancini" line handbag**, natural wicker handle. Ferragamo is known for using unusual materials; straw, raffia and wicker are part of this tradition. This famous and contemporary line of accessories was created at the end of the 1980s. 1996 spring-summer collection. © Photo Giovanni Gastel.

The publisher would like to thank the Salvatore Ferragamo family, along with the house of Salvatore Ferragamo, and especially Stefania Ricci, from the Salvatore Ferragamo Museum in Florence, and Nathalie Morin, from the Parisian house, for their assistance in producing this book.
The author would also like to thank Annie Schneider, who was the first to introduce him to the universe of Salvatore Ferragamo.